The Aesthetic Unconscious

The Aesthetic Unconscious

JACQUES RANCIÈRE

TRANSLATED BY
DEBRA KEATES AND JAMES SWENSON

polity

Ouvrage publié avec le concours du Ministère français de la Culture –
Centre national du livre

Published with the assistance of the French Ministry of Culture –
National Centre for the Book

First published in French as *L'inconscient esthétique*
© Editions Galilée, 2001

This English edition © Polity Press, 2009

Polity Press
65 Bridge Street
Cambridge CB2 1UR, UK

Polity Press
350 Main Street
Malden, MA 02148, USA

ISBN-13: 978-0-7456-4643-5
ISBN-13: 978-0-7456-4644-2(pb)

A catalogue record for this book is available from the British Library.

Designed and typeset in 12/17pt ITC Garamond Light
by Peter Ducker MISTD

Printed and bound in Great Britain
by MPG Books Limited, Bodmin, Cornwall

For further information on Polity, visit our website:
www.politybooks.com

Contents

1 | What Freud Has to Do with Aesthetics

My title does not mean that I intend to talk about the application of the Freudian theory of the unconscious to the domain of aesthetics.[1] I will not be speaking about the psychoanalysis of art, nor about the numerous and significant borrowings that historians and philosophers of art have made from particular theses advanced by Freud or Lacan. I have no particular competence regarding psychoanalytic theory. More importantly, however, my interest lies in a different direction. I am not interested in the application of Freudian concepts to the analysis and interpretation of literary texts or plastic works of art. I will instead ask why the interpretation of these texts and works

[1] This text was originally presented in the form of two lectures, delivered at the "School for Psychoanalyses" in Brussels in January 2000 on the invitation of Didier Cromphout.

occupies such an important, strategic position in Freud's demonstration of the pertinence of analytic concepts and forms of interpretation. I have in mind here not only the books or articles that Freud specifically devoted to writers or artists – to Leonardo da Vinci's biography, Michelangelo's *Moses*, or Jensen's *Gradiva* – but also the references to literary texts and characters that frequently support his demonstrations, such as the multiple references made in the *Interpretation of Dreams* to both the glories of the national literary tradition, such as Goethe's *Faust*, and contemporary works like Alphonse Daudet's *Sapho*.

The reversal of approach proposed here does not imply an intention to turn Freud's questions around against him, in order to ask, for example, why he is interested in Michelangelo's *Moses* or a specific note from Leonardo's *Notebooks* in particular. The members of the analytic profession have already explained to us the circumstances of the father of psychoanalysis's identification with the guardian of the Tables of the Law or the import of his confusion between a kite and a vulture. My

2

goal is not to psychoanalyze Freud and I am not concerned with the way in which the literary and artistic figures he chose fit into the analytic romance of the Founder. What interests me is the question of what these figures serve to prove and what structures allow them to produce this proof.

What these figures serve to prove at the most general level is that there is meaning in what seems not to have any meaning, something enigmatic in what seems self-evident, a spark of thought in what appears to be an anodyne detail. These figures are not the *materials* upon which analytic interpretation proves its ability to interpret cultural formations. They are *testimony* to the existence of a particular relation between thought and non-thought, a particular way that thought is present within sensible materiality, meaning within the insignificant, and an involuntary element within conscious thought. In short, Dr Freud, the interpreter of the "anodyne" facts abandoned by his positivist colleagues, can use these "examples" in his demonstration because they are themselves tokens of a certain unconscious. To

3

put it another way: if it was possible for Freud to formulate the psychoanalytical theory of the unconscious, it was because an unconscious mode of thought had already been identified outside of the clinical domain as such, and the domain of works of art and literature can be defined as the privileged ground where this "unconscious" is at work. My investigation will thus bear upon the way Freudian theory is anchored in this already existing configuration of "unconscious thought," in the idea of the relation between thought and non-thought that was formed and developed primarily in the field of what is called aesthetics. We will therefore inter-pret Freud's "aesthetic" studies as marking the inscription of analytic thought within the horizon of aesthetic thought.

This project naturally presupposes that we come to terms with the notion of aesthetics itself. I do not consider aesthetics to be the name of the science or discipline that deals with art. In my view it designates a mode of thought that develops with respect to things of art and that is concerned to show them to be things of thought. More fundamentally, aesthetics is a particular historical regime of thinking about art and an idea of thought according to which things of art are things of thought. It is well known that the use of the word "aesthetics" to designate thinking about art is recent. Its genealogy is generally referred to in Baumgarten's *Aesthetica*, published in 1750, and Kant's *Critique of Judgment*. But these landmarks are equivocal. For Baumgarten the term "aesthetics" in fact does not designate the theory of art but rather the domain of sensible knowledge, the clear but nonetheless "confused" or indistinct knowledge that can be contrasted with the clear and distinct knowledge of logic. Kant's position in this genealogy is equally problematic. When he borrows the term "aesthetics" from Baumgarten as a name for the theory of forms of sensibility, Kant in fact rejects what gave it its meaning, namely the idea of the sensible as a "confused" intelligible. For Kant it is impossible to conceive of aesthetics as a theory of indistinct knowledge. Indeed, the *Critique of the Faculty of Judgment* does not recognize "aesthetics" as a theory; "aesthetic" only appears as an adjective, and it designates a type of judgment rather than a domain of objects. It is only in the context of Romanticism and post-Kantian idealism – through the writings of Schelling, the Schlegel brothers, and Hegel – that aesthetics comes to designate the thought of art, even as the inappropriateness of the term is constantly remarked. Only in this later context do we see an identification between the thought of art – the thought effectuated by works of art – and a certain idea of "confused knowledge" occur under the name of aesthetics. This new and paradoxical idea makes art the territory of a thought that is present outside itself and identical with non-thought. It unites Baumgarten's definition of the sensible as "confused" idea with Kant's contrary definition of the sensible as heterogeneous to the idea. Henceforth confused knowledge is no longer a lesser form of knowledge but properly *the thought of that which does not think.*[2]

[2] So frequently today one hears deplored the fact that aesthetics has been led astray from its true destination as a critique of the

In other words, "aesthetics" is not a new name for the domain of "art." It is a specific configuration of this domain. It is not the new rubric under which we can group what formerly fell under the general concept of *poetics*. It marks a transformation of the regime of thinking about art. This new regime provides the locus where a specific idea of thought is constituted. My hypothesis in this book is that the Freudian thought of the unconscious is only possible on the basis of this regime of thinking about art and the idea of thought that is immanent to it. Or, if you prefer, Freudian thought, despite the classicism of Freud's artistic references, is only possible on the basis of the revolution that moves the domain of the arts from the reign of poetics to that of aesthetics.

In order to develop and justify these propositions, I will attempt to show the link between a

---

judgment of taste, as Kant had formulated it in a summary of Enlightenment thought. But only what exists can be led astray. Since aesthetics never was the theory of taste, the wish that it might become it once again merely expresses the endless refrain of a "return" to some impossible prerevolutionary paradise of "liberal individualism."

certain number of privileged objects and modes of interpretation in Freudian theory and the changing status of these objects in the *aesthetic* configuration of thinking about art. Giving credit where credit is due, we will begin with the central poetic character in the elaboration of psycho-analysis, Oedipus. In *The Interpretation of Dreams*, Freud explains that there exists "legendary material" whose universal dramatic power rests upon its conformity with the univer-sal data of infant psychology. This material is the Oedipus legend and the eponymous drama by Sophocles.[3] Freud thus hypothesizes that the Oedipal dramatic scheme is universal from a double point of view: as the development of universal – and universally repressed – infantile desires, but also as exemplary form of revelation of a hidden secret. The gradually intensified and

[3] Sigmund Freud, *The Interpretation of Dreams*, in *The Standard Edition of the Complete Psychological Works of Sigmund Freud*, trans. and ed. James Strachey (London: Hogarth, 1953–1974), vol. 4, p. 261. Hereafter cited as *Standard Edition*, with title of indi-vidual work, volume and page numbers.

skillfully delayed revelation of *Oedipus the King* is comparable, says Freud, to the work of psychoanalysis. He thus combines three things within a single affirmation of universality: a general tendency of the human psyche, a determinate fictional material, and an exemplary dramatic schema. The question then becomes, what allows Freud to affirm this adequation and make it the center of his demonstration? In other terms, what are we to make of the universal dramatic power of the Oedipal story and the scheme of revelation employed by Sophocles? The difficult experience of a playwright who attempted to exploit the success of this material will provide the example that will allow us to approach this question.

2 | A Defective Subject

In 1659 Corneille was commissioned to write a tragedy for the festival celebrating Carnival. For the playwright, who had been absent from the stage for seven years following the resounding failure of *Pertharite*, it was the chance for a comeback. He could not afford another failure and only had two months to write his tragedy. The greatest chance at success, he felt, would be provided by the definitive tragic subject. Since it had already been handled by illustrious models he would only have to "translate" and adapt it for the French stage. He therefore chose to do an *Oedipus*. But this golden subject quickly turned out to be a trap. In order to have any chance at the success he was counting on, Corneille had to give up the idea of transposing Sophocles. The schema of revelation and Oedipus's guilt was completely impractical and needed to be reworked.

> I knew that what had passed for miraculous in those long-ago times would seem horrible in our age, and that the eloquent and curious description of the way the unhappy prince puts out his eyes – and the spectacle of the blood from those same dead eyes dripping down his face, which occupies the whole fifth act in the incomparable original version – would offend the delicacy of the ladies who compose the most beautiful portion of our audience and whose disgust would easily entail condemnation by those who accompany them, and finally that, since love plays no part and ladies have no roles in the subject, it was lacking in the principal ornaments that ordinarily win us the approbation of the public.[4]

---

[4] Pierre Corneille, *Œuvres complètes*, ed. Georges Couton (Paris: Gallimard, Bibliothèque de la Pléiade, 1987), vol. 3, pp. 18–19.

Corneille's problems, as you will have noted, did not stem from the theme of incest. They derived from the way the theme is turned into a narrative, from the schema of revelation and the theatrical physicality of the *dénouement*. Three points made the simple transposition that had first been envisaged impossible: the horror of Oedipus's dead eyes, the absence of love interest, and finally the abuse of oracles, which allow the audience to guess the answer to the riddle too easily and make the blindness of the solver of riddles unbelievable.

The Sophoclean schema of the revelation is defective in that it shows too clearly what should only be said and makes known too soon what should remain mysterious. So Corneille had to fix these deficiencies. In order to spare the sensibility of the ladies, he moved off-stage the moment when Oedipus gouges out his eyes. But he put Tiresias off-stage as well. He suppressed the verbal confrontation – so central for Sophocles – between the one who knows but does not want to speak – and tells the truth anyway – and the one who wants to know but refuses to hear the words that reveal the truth he seeks. Corneille replaced this all-too-apparent game of hide-and-seek that the guilty detective plays with the truth with a modern plot, that is, a plot involving a conflict of passions and interests that creates indecision about the identity of the guilty party. The love story lacking in Sophocles' play was necessary in order to produce this conflict and suspense. Corneille gave Oedipus a sister, Dircé, whom he deprived of the throne that was hers by right, and gave Dircé a lover, Theseus. Since Dircé thinks she is responsible for the journey that cost her father his life, and Theseus has doubts about his own birth (or at least he pretends to in order to protect the woman he loves), three interpretations of the oracle become possible and three characters could turn out to be guilty. The love story preserves suspense and uncertainty about the *dénouement* through careful handling of the distribution of knowledge.

Sixty years later, another playwright encountered the same problem and resolved it in much the same way. At the age of twenty, Voltaire chose the subject of Oedipus to start his career as a dramatist. But he did so on the basis of an even more direct criticism of Sophocles than that of Corneille, denouncing the "improbabilities" of the plot of *Oedipus the King*. It is unbelievable that Oedipus does not know the circumstances in which his predecessor Laios died. It is equally unbelievable that he does not understand what Tiresias says to him and that he insults the man whom he had brought before him as a venerable prophet and calls him a liar. The conclusion drawn by Voltaire is radical: "It is a defect in the subject, people say, and not one introduced by the author. As if it were not the author's job to correct his subject when it is defective!"[5] Voltaire therefore corrected his subject by finding another candidate for Laios's murder: Philoctetes, formerly an exposed child, desperately in love with Jocasta, who had disappeared from Thebes at the time of the murder and returns precisely at the time a guilty party is needed.

[5] Voltaire, *Lettres sur Œdipe*, in *Œuvres complètes* (Oxford: The Voltaire Foundation, 2001), vol. 1A, p. 337

A "defective subject" is thus how the classical age, the age of representation, saw the workings of Sophoclean psychoanalysis. This deficiency, we must emphasize again, is not due to the incest story. The difficulties Corneille and Voltaire encountered in adapting Sophocles provide no grist for an argument against the universality of the Oedipus complex. What they do put into doubt, on the other hand, is the universality of Oedipal "psychoanalysis," that is, Sophocles' scenario for the revelation of the secret. For Corneille and Voltaire this scenario established a defective relation between what is seen and what is said, between what is said and what is understood. Too much is shown to the spectator. This excess, moreover, is not merely a question of the disgusting spectacle of the gouged-out eyes; it concerns the mark of thought upon the body more generally. Above all, the scenario allows too much to be understood. Contrary to what Freud says, there is no proper suspense and skillful progression in the unveiling of truth to both the hero and the spectator. What then compromises this dramatic rationality? There can be no doubt: it is the "subject," the character of Oedipus himself. It is the fury that compels him to want to know at any cost, against all and against himself, and, at the same time, not to understand the barely veiled words that offer him the truth he demands. Here lies the heart of the problem: Oedipus, driven mad by his need for knowledge, does not merely upset the "delicacy" of the ladies when he gouges out his eyes. What he upsets, in the end, is the order of the representative system that gives dramatic creation its rule.

Essentially two things are meant by the order of representation. In the first place it is a certain order of relations between what can be said and what can be seen. The essence of speech in this order is to show. But speech shows within the bounds of a double restraint. On the one hand, the function of visible manifestation restrains the power of speech. Speech makes manifest senti-ments and wills rather than speaking on its own, as the speech of Tiresias – like that of Sophocles or Aeschylus – does in an oracular or enigmatic mode. On the other hand, this function restrains the power of the visible itself. Speech institutes a certain visibility: it makes manifest what is hidden in souls, recounts and describes what is far from one's eyes. But in so doing it restrains the visible that it makes manifest under its command. It forbids the visible from showing on its own, from showing the unspeakable, the horror of the gouged-out eyes.

In the second place the order of representation is a certain order of relations between knowledge and action. Drama, says Aristotle, is an arrangement of actions. At the base of drama are characters who pursue particular ends while acting in conditions of partial ignorance, which will be resolved in the course of the action. What this excludes is what constitutes the very ground of the Oedipal performance, namely the *pathos* of knowledge: the maniacal, relentless determination to know what it would be better not to know, the furor that prevents understanding, the refusal to recognize the truth in the form in which it presents itself, the catastrophe of unsustainable knowing, a knowing that obliges one to withdraw from the world of visibility. Sophocles' tragedy is made from this *pathos*. Already Aristotle no longer understands it and represses it behind the theory of dramatic action that makes knowing a result of the ingenious machinery of reversal and recognition. It is this *pathos* that, in the classical age, makes Oedipus an impossible hero unless radical corrections are made. Impossible not because he kills his father and sleeps with his mother, but because of the way that he learns about it, because of the identity of opposites that he incarnates in this learning, the tragic identity of knowing and not knowing, of action undertaken and *pathos* undergone.

3 | The Aesthetic Revolution

It is thus a whole regime of thinking about poetry that rejects the Oedipal scenario. We can put this the other way around: the Oedipal scenario can only acquire a privileged status after the abolition of the representative regime of thinking about the arts, a regime that implies a certain idea of thought: thought as action imposing itself upon a passive matter. This is precisely what I have called the aesthetic revolution: the end of an ordered set of relations between what can be seen and what can be said, knowledge and action, activity and passivity. For Oedipus to be the hero of the psychoanalytic revolution, then, there must first be a new Oedipus, one who has nothing to do with those imagined by Corneille and Voltaire. Beyond French-style tragedy, beyond even the Aristotelian rationalization of tragic action, this new Oedipus seeks to restore the tragic thought of Sophocles. Hölderlin, Hegel, and Nietzsche were among those who put forth this new Oedipus and the new idea of tragedy that corresponds to him.

Two traits characterize this new Oedipus and make him the hero of a "new" idea of thought that claims to revive the idea of thought attested to by Greek tragedy. Oedipus is proof of a certain existential savagery of thought, a definition of knowing not as the subjective act of grasping an objective ideality but as the affection, passion, or even sickness of a living being. The signification of the Oedipal story according to *The Birth of Tragedy* is that knowledge in itself is a crime against nature.[6] Oedipus and tragedy generally attest to the fact that, in the matter of thought, there is always a question of sickness, medicine, and their paradoxical unity. This philosophical restaging of the tragic equivalence between

---

[6] Friedrich Nietzsche, *The Birth of Tragedy*, ed. Raymond Geuss and Ronald Speirs (Cambridge: Cambridge University Press, 1999), pp. 47–8.

knowing and suffering (the *pathei mathos* of Aeschylus or Sophocles) presupposes a gathering of the trio of those who are sick with knowing: Oedipus and Hamlet, together in *The Interpretation of Dreams* as they were in Hegel's *Lectures on Aesthetics*, and Faust who is there as well. The invention of psychoanalysis occurs at the point where philosophy and medicine put each other into question by making thought a matter of sickness and sickness a matter of thought.

But this solidarity between the things of thought and the things of sickness is itself in solidarity with the new regime of thinking about the productions of art. If Oedipus is an exemplary hero, it is because his fictional figure emblematizes the properties given to the productions of art by the aesthetic revolution. Oedipus is he who knows and does not know, who is absolutely active and absolutely passive. Such an identity of contraries is precisely how the aesthetic revolution defines what is proper to art. At first sight, it seems only to set an absolute capacity for creation in opposition to the norms of the representative regime. The work now stands under its own law of production and is its own proof. But at the same time this unconditional creativity is identified with an absolute passivity. Kant's conception of genius summarizes this duality. The genius is the active power of nature who sets his own creative power against any model or norm. The genius, we might say, becomes a norm for himself. But at the same time he is the one who does not know what he does and is incapable of accounting for his own activity.

This identity between knowing and not knowing, between activity and passivity, is the very fact of art in the aesthetic regime; it radicalizes what Baumgarten called "confused clarity" into an identity of contraries. In this sense, the aesthetic revolution had already begun in the eighteenth century when Vico undertook to establish, in his *New Science*, the figure of what he called the "true Homer," in opposition to Aristotle and the entire representative tradition. It is worth recalling the context in order to clarify the filiation that interests us. Vico's primary target is not the "theory of art" but the old theologico-poetic business about the "wisdom of the Egyptians." This question of whether hieroglyphic language was a code in which religious wisdom forbidden to the uninitiated has been deposited, and likewise whether ancient poetic fables were the allegorical expression of philosophical thought, dates back at least to Plato. In denouncing the immorality of the Homeric fables, Plato in effect refuted those who saw cosmological allegories in the divine adulteries they narrated. The question reappears in the proto-Christian era, when pagan authors, seeking to refute the accusation of idolatry, once again promote the idea of wisdom encrypted in ideogrammatic writing and the fables of the poets. It returns with force in the seventeenth and eighteenth centuries, borne by both the development of exegetical methods and the philosophical quarrel over the origins of language. Within this context Vico seeks to kill two birds with one stone. He hopes to liquidate the idea of a mysterious wisdom hidden in imagistic writing and poetic fables. In opposition to this search for

hidden meanings he proposes a new hermeneutics that instead relates the image to the conditions
of its production. But at the same time he demol-
ishes the traditional image of the poet as the
inventor of fables, characters, and images. His
discovery of the "true Homer" refutes the Aristotelian and representative image of the poet as
inventor of fables, characters, images, and rhymes
on four points. First, he shows, Homer is not an
inventor of fables. He did not recognize our
distinction between history and fiction, and in fact
considered his so-called fables to be history,
which he transmitted as he had received them.
Secondly, he is not the inventor of characters. His
so-called characters, Achilles the brave, Ulysses
the clever, Nestor the wise, are neither individual-
ized characters nor allegories invented for poetic
purposes. They are abstractions in images, which
are the only way for a thought that is equally incapable of abstraction and individualization to represent virtues – courage, intelligence, wisdom, or
justice – that it cannot conceive nor even name as
such. Thirdly, Homer is not the much-celebrated

inventor of beautiful metaphors and brilliant images. He simply lived in an age when thought could not be separated from the image nor the abstract from the concrete. His "images" are nothing but the way people of his time spoke. Finally, he is not the inventor of rhythms and meters. He is simply proof of a stage of language in which speech and song were identical. Men sang before speaking, before passing to articulated language. The poetic charms of sung speech are actually only the stammerings of language's infancy, still observable in the language of deaf-mutes. Thus the four traditional privileges of the poet-inventor are transformed into properties of his language. This language is his only insofar as it does not belong to him; it is not an instrument at his disposal but the token of an infantile stage of language, thought, and humanity. Homer is a poet on account of the identity between what he wants and what he does not want, what he knows and what he does not know, what he does and what he does not do. The existence of poetry is tied to this identity of contraries, to this gap between

27

speech and what it says. There is solidarity between the poetic character of language and its ciphered character. But this cipher does not hide any secret science. It is in the end nothing more than the inscription of the process that produces speech itself.

This hermeneutical figure of the "true Homer" is a prerequisite to the figure of Oedipus as an exemplary and universally valid tragic subject. This figure presupposes a regime of thinking about art in which art is defined by its being the identity of a conscious procedure and an unconscious production, of a willed action and an involuntary process. In short, the identity of *logos* and *pathos* will henceforth be what attests to the existence of art. But there are two contrary ways to think about this identity: as the immanence of *logos* in *pathos*, of thought in non-thought, or, inversely, as the immanence of *pathos* in *logos*, of non-thought in thought. We find the first manner illustrated in the great founding texts of the aesthetic mode of thought such as Hegel's *Lectures on Aesthetics*. Art, in Schelling's terms, is a spirit's odyssey outside of itself. In Hegel's systematization, this spirit seeks to become manifest, which means in the first place to make itself manifest to itself, through the matter that is its opposite: in the compactness of built or sculpted stone, in the density of color or in the temporal and sonorous materiality of language. It seeks itself in the double sensible exteriority of matter and the image. It seeks itself and misses itself. But in this game of hide-and-seek, it creates itself as the interior light of sensible materiality, the beautiful appearance of the god of stone, the arborescent thrust of the Gothic vault and spire, or the spiritual brilliance animating the still-life's insignificance. The inverse model that can be opposed to this odyssey is that of the beautiful and rational aesthetic appearance whose obscure depths are riven with pathos. In Schopenhauer this model is expressed by the movement that turns its back on the appearances and the lovely causal order of the world of representation in order to face the obscure, subterranean and nonsensical world of the thing-in-itself: the meaningless world of naked will-to-life, of the paradoxically named "will" whose essence is to want nothing, rejecting the model of the choice of ends and the adaptation of means to those ends that forms the usual meaning of the notion of will. In Nietzsche it is expressed by the identification of the existence of art itself with the polarity of Apollonian beautiful appearance and the Dionysian drive that brings joy and suffering in equal measure and comes to light in the very forms that would deny its existence.

4 | The Two Forms of Mute Speech

Psychoanalysis thus finds its historical birthplace within this counter-movement whose philosophical heroes are Schopenhauer and the young Nietzsche and which reigns in the literature that, from Zola to Maupassant, Ibsen, or Strindberg, plunges into the pure meaninglessness of raw life or into the encounter with the powers of darkness. We are not merely concerned with the influence of the spirit of the age; more precisely, we are trying to establish the positions possible within a system as defined by a certain idea of thought and a certain idea of writing. For the silent revolution that we have called aesthetic opens the space in which an idea of thought and a corresponding idea of writing can be elaborated. This idea of thought rests upon a fundamental affirmation: there is thought that does not think, thought at work not only in the foreign element of non-thought but in the very form of non-thought. Conversely, there is non-thought that inhabits thought and gives it a power all its own. This non-thought is not simply a form of absence of thought, it is an efficacious presence of its opposite. From whichever side we approach the equation, the identity of thought and non-thought is the source of a distinctive power.

Corresponding to this idea of thought is an idea of writing. Writing refers not only to a form of manifestation of speech but more fundamentally to an idea of speech itself and its intrinsic power. It is well known that for Plato writing designated not only the materiality of the written sign on a material support, but a specific status of speech. He considered writing to be a mute *logos*, speech that is incapable of saying what it says differently or of choosing not to speak. It can neither account for what it proffers nor discern those whom it is or is not appropriate to address. This speech, simultaneously mute and chatty, can be contrasted with speech that is action, discourse guided by a signification to be transmitted and a goal to be achieved. For Plato this was the speech of the master who knows how to explain his words and how to hold them in reserve, how to keep them away from the profane and how to deposit them like seed in the souls of those in whom they can bear fruit. The classical representative order identified this "living speech" with the active speech of the great orator who moves deeply and persuades, edifies and leads souls and bodies. This model likewise includes the discourse of the tragic hero who pursues his will and his passions to the limit.

In opposition to this living speech that provided the representative order with its norm, writing is the mode of speech that corresponds to the aesthetic revolution: the contradictory mode of a speech that speaks and keeps silent at the same time, that both knows and does not know what it is saying. But there are two major figures of this contradictory mode, corresponding to the two opposite forms of the relation between thought and non-thought. The polarity of these two figures sketches out the space of a single domain, that of literary speech as symptomatic speech.[7]

Mute writing, in the first sense, is the speech borne by mute things themselves. It is the capability of signification that is inscribed upon their very body, summarized by the "everything speaks" of Novalis, the poet-mineralogist. Everything is trace, vestige, or fossil. Every sensible form, beginning from the stone or the shell, tells a story. In their striations and ridges they all bear the traces of their history and the mark of their destination. Literature takes up the task of deciphering and rewriting these signs of history written on things. Balzac summarizes and celebrates this new idea of writing in the decisive pages at the beginning of *The Wild Ass's Skin* that describe the antiquary's store as the emblem of a new mythology, a phantasmagoria formed entirely from the ruins of consumption. The great poet of the new age is not Byron, the reporter of the

[7] See Jacques Rancière, *La Parole muette: Essai sur les contradictions de la littérature* (Paris: Hachette, 1998).

soul's turmoil. It is Cuvier the geologist, the naturalist who reconstitutes animal populations from bones and forests from fossilized imprints.[8] With him a new idea of the artist is defined as one who travels through the labyrinths and crypts of the social world. He gathers the vestiges and transcribes the hieroglyphs painted in the configuration of obscure or random things. He gives the insignificant details of the prose of the world their power of poetic signification. In the topography of a plaza, the physiognomy of a facade, the pattern or wear of a piece of clothing, the chaos of a pile of merchandise or trash, he recognizes the elements of a mythology. He makes the true history of a society, an age, or a people visible in the figures of this mythology, foreshadowing individual or collective destiny. *Everything speaks* implies the abolition of the hierarchies of the representative order. The great Freudian rule that there are no insignificant "details" – that on the contrary it is the details that put us on the path of

8 Honoré de Balzac, *The Wild Ass's Skin*, trans. Herbert J. Hunt (Harmondsworth: Penguin, 1977), p. 41.

truth – is in direct continuity with the aesthetic revolution. There are no noble and vulgar subjects, nor important narrative episodes and accessory descriptive ones. There is not a single episode, description, or sentence that does not bear within itself the signifying power of the entire work. There is nothing that does not bear the power of language. Everything is on an equal footing, equally important, equally significant. Thus the narrator of *At the Sign of the Cat and Racket* sets us in front of the facade of a house whose asymmetrical openings, chaotic recesses and outcroppings form a tissue of hieroglyphs in which we can decipher the history of the house – the history of the society to which it bears witness – and the destiny of the characters who live there. Similarly, *Les Misérables* plunges us into the sewer that, like a cynic philosopher, says everything; it brings together on an equal basis everything that civilization uses and throws away, its masks and its distinctions as well as its everyday utensils. The new poet, the geological or archeological poet, performs the same sort of inquiry that Freud conducts in *The Interpretation of Dreams.* He poses the principle that nothing is insignificant, that the prosaic details that positivistic thought disdains or attributes to a merely physiological rationality are in fact signs encrypting a history. But he also poses the paradoxical condition of this hermeneutics: in order for the banal to reveal its secret, it must first be mythologized. The house and the sewer speak, they bear the trace of truth – as will the dream or the parapraxis, and the Marxian commodity – insofar as they are first transformed into the elements of a mythology or phantasmagoria.

The writer is thus a geologist or archeologist exploring the labyrinths of the social world, and later those of the self. He gathers remnants, exhumes fossils, and transcribes signs that bear witness to a world and write a history. The mute writing of things delivers, in its prose, the truth of a civilization or an age that the once-glorious scene of "living speech" had hidden from view. The latter has now become a vain scene of oratory, the discourse of superficial agitations. But

the interpreter of signs is also a doctor, a sympto-
matologist who diagnoses the illnesses afflicting
the enterprising individual and the brilliant society. The naturalist and geologist Balzac is also a
doctor able to detect, at the heart of the intense
activity of individuals and societies, a sickness
identical to this intensity. In Balzac's work the
name for this sickness is *will*: the malady of
thought that seeks to transform itself into reality
and so carries individuals and societies toward
their destruction. Indeed, the history of nine-
teenth-century literature can be described as the
history of the transformations of the "will." In the
naturalist and symbolist period, it will become
impersonal destiny, heredity, the accomplishment
of a will-to-live devoid of reason, an assault upon
the illusions of consciousness by the world of
obscure forces. Literary symptomatology will then
acquire a new status in this literature of the
pathologies of thought centering on hysteria,
"nervosism," or the weight of the past. These new
dramaturgies of the buried secret trace the life-
history of the individual in order to uncover the

profound secret of heredity and race and, in the final instance, the naked and meaningless fact of life.

This literature is attached to the second form of identity of *logos* and *pathos* mentioned above, the one following an inverse path from the clear to the obscure and from *logos* to *pathos*, to the pure suffering of existence and the pure reproduction of the meaninglessness of life. A second form of mute speech is likewise at work here. In place of the hieroglyph inscribed on the body and subject to deciphering we encounter speech as soliloquy, speaking to no one and saying nothing but the impersonal and unconscious conditions of speech itself. In Freud's time it was Maeterlinck who most forcefully theorized this second form of mute speech, of unconscious discourse, in his analysis of "second-degree dialogue" in Ibsen's dramas.[9] This dialogue expresses not the thoughts, sentiments, and intentions of the characters, but the

[9] Maurice Maeterlinck, "The Tragical in Daily Life," in *The Treasure of the Humble*, trans. Alfred Sutro (New York: Dodd, Mead, and Co., n.d.), pp. 113–35.

thought of the "third person" who haunts the dialogue, the confrontation with the Unknown, with the anonymous and meaningless forces of life. The "language of motionless tragedy" transcribes "the unconscious movements of a being reaching luminous hands through the battlements of the artificial fortress in which we are imprisoned,"[10] the knocking of "a hand that does not belong to us [and] strikes the secret gates of our instinct."[11] These doors, says Maeterlinck in sum, cannot be opened, but we can listen to the "knocking behind the door." We can transpose the dramatic poem, formerly dedicated to an

[10] Jules Huret, "Conversation avec Maurice Maeterlinck," and Maeterlinck, "Confession de poète," in Maeterlinck, *Introduction à une psychologie des songes et autres écrits* (Brussels: Labor, 1986), pp. 156 and 81.

[11] Maeterlinck, "Small Talk: The Theater," in *Symbolist Art Theories: A Critical Anthology*, ed. Henri Dorra (Berkeley: University of California Press, 1995), p. 144. I am well aware that Maeterlinck places himself in the lineage of Emerson and the mystical tradition, not in that of Schopenhauerian "nihilism." But what interests me here – and what moreover makes possible the confusion of the two traditions – is the same status they give to voiceless speech as the expression of an unconscious "willing" of existence.

"arrangement of actions," into the language of these blows, the speech of the invisible crowd that haunts our thoughts. Perhaps what the stage needs is for this speech to be incarnated in a new body: no longer the human body of the actor/character but that of a being "who would appear to live without being alive," a body of shadow or wax granted to this multiple and anonymous voice.[12] From this Maeterlinck draws the idea of an android theater that links Villiers de L'Isle-Adam's novelistic reverie with the future of the theater, from Edward Gordon Craig's Über-Marionette to Tadeusz Kantor's *Dead Class*.

The aesthetic unconscious, consubstantial with the aesthetic regime of art, manifests itself in the polarity of this double scene of mute speech: on the one hand, a speech written on the body that must be restored to a linguistic signification by a labor of deciphering and rewriting; on the other, the voiceless speech of a nameless power that lurks behind any consciousness and any signification, to

[12] Maeterlinck, "Small Talk," p. 145.

which voice and body must be given. The cost, however, may be that this anonymous voice and ghostly body lead the human subject down the path of the great renunciation toward the nothingness of will whose Schopenhauerian shadow weighs so heavily on the literature of the unconscious.

5 | From One Unconscious to Another

The goal of this outline of the literary and philosophical figure of the aesthetic unconscious, it may bear repeating, is not to provide the model for a new genealogy of the Freudian unconscious. We have no intention of forgetting the medical and scientific context in which psychoanalysis was elaborated, nor of dissolving the Freudian concept of the unconscious, the economy of the drives, and the study of the formations of the unconscious in a century-old idea of unknown knowing and thought that does not think. Nor is there any point in trying to turn the game around and show how the Freudian unconscious is unconsciously dependent on the literature and art whose hidden secrets it claims to unveil. What matters is rather to point out the relations of complicity and conflict established between the

aesthetic unconscious and the Freudian unconscious. We can define the stakes of the encounter
between these two versions of the unconscious
on the basis of Freud's own indications when he
recounts the invention of psychoanalysis in *The
Interpretation of Dreams*. His narrative posits a
contrast between psychoanalysis and the notion
of science associated with positivistic medicine,
which treats the peculiarities of the sleeping mind
as negligible data or attributes them to deter-
minable physical causes. In his battle against this
sort of positivism, Freud calls on psychoanalysis
to forge an alliance with the old mythological
heritage and popular belief concerning the signification of dreams. But there is another alliance
woven into *The Interpretation of Dreams*, which
will become more explicit in the book on
Gradiva: an alliance with Goethe and Schiller,
Sophocles and Shakespeare, as well as other writers, less prestigious but nearer to him, such as
Popper-Lynkeus and Alphonse Daudet. Freud is
doubtless playing the authority of the great names
of culture off against those of the masters of

science. But, more fundamentally, these great names function as guides in the journey across the Acheron undertaken by the new science. If guides are necessary, it is precisely because the space between positive science and popular belief or legend is not empty. The aesthetic unconscious took possession of this domain by redefining the things of art as specific modes of union between the thought that thinks and the thought that does not think. It is occupied by the literature of travel into the depths, of the hermeneutics of mute signs and the transcription of voiceless speech. This literature has already created a link between the poetic practice of displaying and interpreting signs and a particular idea of civilization, its brilliant appearances and obscure depths, it sicknesses and the medicines appropriate to them. This idea is not limited to the naturalist novel's interest in hysterics and the syndromes of degeneration. The elaboration of a new medicine and science of the *psyche* is possible because a whole domain of thought and writing separates science and superstition. But the

45

fact that this semiological and symptomatological scene has its own consistency makes any simply utilitarian alliance between Freud and writers or artists impossible. The literature to which Freud refers has its own idea of the unconscious, the *pathos* of thought, and the maladies and medicines of civilization. Pragmatic utilization is no more possible than unconscious continuity. The domain of thought that does not think is not a realm where Freud appears as a solitary explorer in search of companions and allies. It is an already occupied territory where one unconscious enters into competition and conflict with another.

In order to grasp this twofold relation, we must pose the question again in its most general form: what business does Freud have in the history of art? The question is itself double. What pushes Freud to make himself into a historian or analyst of art? What is at stake in the full-scale analyses that he devotes to Leonardo, to Michelangelo's *Moses* or Jensen's *Gradiva*, or in his shorter remarks on Hoffmann's *Sandman* or Ibsen's *Rosmersholm*? Why these examples? What is he

46

looking for in them and how does he treat them? This first series of questions, as we have seen, implies another: how should we think of Freud's place in the history of art? Not only the place of Freud as an "analyst of art," but of Freud the scientist, the doctor of the *psyche*, interpreter of its formations and their disturbances? The "history of art" in this sense is something quite different from the succession of works and movements. It is the history of regimes of thinking about art, that is, of particular ways connecting practices to modes of making those practices visible and thinkable. In the end this means a history of ideas of thought itself.[13] The double question can then be reformulated as follows: what is Freud looking for and what does he find in the analysis of the works or thought of artists? What link does the idea of unconscious thought that animates these analyses have with the one that defines a historical regime, the aesthetic regime of art?

[13] See on this point Jacques Rancière, *The Politics of Aesthetics: The Distribution of the Sensible*, trans. Gabriel Rockhill (London: Continuum, 2004).

We can pose these questions on the basis of two theoretical signposts. The first is posed by Freud himself, the second derived from the works and characters privileged by his analysis. As we have seen, Freud affirms that there is an objective alliance between the psychoanalyst and the artist, and particularly between the psychoanalyst and the poet. "Creative writers are valuable allies," he asserts at the beginning of *Delusions and Dreams in Jensen's* Gradiva.[14] Their knowledge of the *psyche*, the singular formations and hidden operations of the human mind, is ahead of that of the scientists. They know things that the scientists do not, for they are aware of the importance and rationality proper to this phantasmatic component that positive science either sees as chimerical nothingness or attributes to simple physical or physiological causes. Poets and novelists are thus the allies of the psychoanalyst, the scientist who sees all the manifestations of the mind as equally important and knows there is a profound rationality to its "fancies," aberrations, and

[14] Sigmund Freud, *Delusions and Dreams in Jensen's "Gradiva," Standard Edition*, vol. 9, p. 8.

non-sense. This important point is too often underestimated: Freud's approach to art is not in the least motivated by a desire to demystify the sublimities of poetry and art and reduce them to the sexual economy of the drives. His goal is not to exhibit the dirty (or stupid) little secret behind the grand myth of creation. Rather, Freud calls on art and poetry to bear positive witness on behalf of the profound rationality of "fantasy" (*fantaisie*) and lend support to a science that claims, in a certain way, to put fantasy, poetry, and mythology back within the fold of scientific rationality. This is why the declaration of alliance is immediately accompanied by a reproach: the poets and novelists are in fact only half-allies. They have not given enough credence to the rationality of dreams and fancy, not taken a clear enough stand on behalf of the meaningfulness of the fantasies they have portrayed.

The second signpost is provided by the figures chosen as examples by Freud. A certain number of them are drawn from contemporary literature, from the naturalist drama of destiny as found in

Ibsen or from a fantastic tradition exemplified by Jensen or Popper-Lynkeus and reaching back to Jean-Paul, Tieck, and Hoffmann. But these contemporary works stand in the shadow of a few great models. First are the two great incarnations of the Renaissance: Michelangelo, the somber demiurge of colossal creations, and Leonardo da Vinci, the artist/scientist/inventor, the man of great dreams and great projects, whose handful of realized works appear as the various figures of a single enigma. Then there are the two romantic heroes of tragedy. Oedipus bears witness to a savage antiquity that stands in sharp contrast with the polite and polished antiquity represented in French tragedy and to a *pathos* of thought that overturns the representative logic of the arrangement of actions and its harmonious distribution of what can be seen and what can be said. Hamlet is the modern hero of a thought that does not act, or rather, a thought that acts by its very inertia. In short, in opposition to the classical order, there is the hero of savage antiquity as celebrated by Hölderlin or Nietzsche, and the heroes of the savage Renaissance, that of Shakespeare but also that studied by Burckhardt or Taine. As we have seen, the classical order is not simply the etiquette of a French-style courtly art. It is properly speaking the representative regime of art, the regime whose first theoretical legitimation is found in Aristotle's elaboration of the notion of *mimesis*, its emblem in classical French tragedy, and its systematization in the great treatises of the French eighteenth century, from Batteux to La Harpe by way of Voltaire's *Commentaires sur Corneille*. At the heart of this regime was a conception of the poem as an ordered arrangement of actions moving toward resolution by way of a confrontation between characters who pursue conflicting goals and manifest their wills and sentiments in their speech following a system of rules of suitability. This system submitted knowledge to the authority of history and visibility to the authority of speech in a relation of mutual restraint between what can be seen and what can be said. It is this order that is split apart by the romantic Oedipus, the hero of a thought that does not know what it knows, wants what it does not want, acts by suffering and speaks through muteness. If Oedipus – and the whole lineage of great Oedipal heroes along with him – is at the center of the Freudian elaboration, it is because he is the emblem of this regime of art that identifies the things of art as things of thought insofar as they are tokens of a thought that is immanent in its other and inhabited by that other, that is everywhere written in the language of sensible signs and withdrawn into its own obscure heart.

6 | Freud's Corrections

As Freud makes an appeal to artists, he remains on the other hand objectively dependent upon the presuppositions of a determinate regime of art. We now need to understand the specificity of the connection between these two facts, which constitutes the specificity of Freud's intervention with respect to the aesthetic unconscious. His primary goal, as we have already noted, is not to establish a sexual etiology for artistic phenomena, but rather to intervene within the notion of unconscious thought that provides the productions of the aesthetic regime of art with their norm. Freud seeks, that is, to reestablish proper order in the way art and the thought of art situate the relations between knowing and not-knowing, sense and non-sense, *logos* and *pathos*, the real and the fantastic. His intervention is first of all designed to discredit an interpretation of these relations that plays upon the ambiguity of the real and the fantastic or sense and non-sense and leads the thought of art and the interpretation of the manifestations of "fantasy" toward a pure and definitive affirmation of *pathos*, of the brute meaninglessness of life. He wants to contribute to the victory of a hermeneutic and explanatory vocation of art over the nihilist entropy inherent in the aesthetic configuration of art.

In order to understand this, we need to compare preliminary remarks made by Freud in two different texts. At the beginning of *The Moses of Michelangelo*, Freud explains that he is not interested in artworks from a formal perspective but in their "subject-matter," in the intention that is expressed and the content that is revealed.[15] At the beginning of the *Gradiva* he reproaches poets for their ambiguity with respect to the signification of the mind's "fantasies." We cannot understand Freud's declared choice of the "content"

[15] Freud, *The Moses of Michelangelo, Standard Edition*, vol. 13, pp. 211–12.

alone of works unless we see it in relation to the second position. The quest for the content, as we know, generally leads toward the discovery of a repressed memory and, in the final instance, toward the original moment of infantile castration anxiety. This assignation of a final cause is generally mediated through an organizing fantasy (*fantasme*), a compromise formation that allows the artist's libido (most often represented by the hero) to escape repression and sublimate itself in the work at the cost of inscribing its enigma there. This overwhelming preconception has the singular consequence of transforming fiction into biography. Freud interprets the fantastic dreams and nightmares of Jensen's Norbert Hanold, Hoffmann's Nathaniel, and Ibsen's Rebecca West as if they were pathological data pertaining to real people, and judges the writer according to the lucidity of the analysis he gives of them. The limit-example is found in a note to the discussion of *The Sandman* in *The Uncanny* where Freud adduces the proof that the optician Coppola and the lawyer Coppelius are one and the same person, namely the castrating father. He thus reestablishes the etiology of Nathaniel's case. In his role as a fantasy doctor, Hoffmann blurred this etiology, but not to the point of hiding it from his knowledgeable colleague, for "Hoffmann's imaginative treatment [*Phantasie*] of his material has not made such wild confusion of its elements that we cannot reconstruct their original arrangement."[16] There thus exists an original arrangement of the "case of Nathaniel." Behind what the writer presents as the product of his unfettered imagination, we must recognize the logic of the fantasy (*fantasme*) and the primal anxiety that it disguises: little Nathaniel's castration anxiety, an expression of the familial drama experienced by Hoffmann himself as a child.

The same procedure runs through the whole book on *Gradiva*. Behind the "arbitrary decision" and the fantastic story of this young man who has fallen in love with a figure of stone and dream to the point of being unable to see the real woman

16 Freud, "The 'Uncanny," *Standard Edition*, vol. 17, p. 232 note.

as anything more than a phantasmatic apparition of this antique figure, Freud attempts to reestablish the true etiology of the case of Norbert Hanold: the repression and displacement of the adolescent's sexual attraction for young Zoe. This correction obliges Freud to found his reasoning on the less than firmly established fact of the "real" existence of a fictional creation. But more importantly it requires a mode of dream interpretation that seems slightly naive with respect to Freud's own scientific principles. The hidden message is in fact provided by a simple translation of the dream figure into its real equivalent: *you are interested in Gradiva because in reality it is Zoe you are interested in.* This synopsis shows that something more than just the reduction of the fictional to a clinical syndrome is going on here. Freud even calls into doubt what might make the syndrome interesting for a doctor, namely the diagnosis of fetishistic erotomania. He further neglects what might interest the scholar concerned with relating clinical practice to the history of myth, namely the long history of myths, exemplified by Pygmalion, about men who fall in love with images and dream of actually possessing them. Only one thing seems to interest Freud: reestablishing linear causality in the plot, even if this requires him to refer to the unverifiable facts of Norbert Hanold's childhood. Even more than the correct explanation of Hanold's case, his concern is to refute the status that Jensen's book gives to literature's "inventions." His refutation bears on two fundamental and complementary points: first, the author's affirmation that the fantasies (*fantasmes*) he describes are the sole invention of his fanciful imagination (*fantaisie*); second, the moral that the author gives to his story, namely the simple triumph of "real life," in flesh and blood and good old plain German, which through the voice of its homonym Zoe mocks the folly of the scholar Norbert and sets its simple and joyous perpetuity in contrast with his idealistic reveries. The author's insistence upon the freedom of his imagination is obviously of a piece with his denunciation of his hero's reveries. This congruence can be summarized by a single Freudian term, desublimation. If there is desublimation going on here, it is the novelist and not the psychoanalyst who carries it out. And it coincides with his "lack of seriousness" with respect to the phantasmatic fact.

Behind the "reduction" of the fictional datum to a non-existent pathological and sexual "reality" is thus a polemic seeking to refute the confusion of the fictional and the real that grounds the practice and the discourse of the novelist. By insisting that the fantasy is the product of his fancy and refuting his character's reverie in the name of the reality principle, the novelist grants himself the capacity to circulate freely on both sides of the boundary between reality and fiction. Freud's first concern is to assert a univocal story against such equivocity. The important point that justifies all the shortcuts of the interpretation is the identification of the love plot with a schema of causal rationality. It is not the final cause – the unverifiable repression going back to Norbert's childhood – that interests Freud so much as causal concatenation as such. It matters little whether the story is real or fictive.

The essential is that it be univocal, that, in contrast to Romanticism's rendering the imaginary and the real indiscernible and reversible, it set forth an Aristotelian arrangement of action and knowledge directed toward the event of recognition.

7 | On Various Uses of Detail

Here the relation between Freudian interpretation and the aesthetic revolution begins to get complicated. Psychoanalysis is possible on the basis of the regime of art that delegitimizes the representative age's well-ordered plots and in turn grants legitimacy to the *pathos* of knowledge. But Freud makes a distinct choice within the configuration of the aesthetic unconscious. He privileges and valorizes the first form of mute speech, that of the symptom that is the trace of a history, in opposition to the other form, that of the anonymous voice of unconscious and meaningless life. This opposition leads him to try to recapture the Romantic figures of the equivalence of *logos* and *pathos* within the old representative logic. The most striking example is to be found in the text on Michelangelo's *Moses*. The object of this analysis is in fact quite unique. Freud does not talk here, as he did in the text on Leonardo, about a fantasy found in a note. He talks about a sculptural work that, he says, he has returned to see several times. His analysis is based an exemplary adequation between visual attention to the work's detail and the psychoanalytic privilege given to "insignificant" details. As is well known, this relation passes by way of an endlessly commented reference to Morelli/Lermolieff, the doctor who became an expert in artworks and the inventor of a forensic method of identifying works on the basis of slight and inimitable details that reveal the artist's individual touch. A method of reading works is thus identified with a paradigm for research into causes. But this detail-oriented method can itself be practiced in two ways, which correspond to the two major forms of the aesthetic unconscious. There is on the one hand the model of the trace that is made to speak, in which the sedimented inscription of a history can be read. In a famous text, Carlo Ginzburg has shown how the reference to Morelli's "method" inscribes Freudian interpretation

in the great judicial paradigm that seeks to recon-
stitute a process on the basis of its traces.[17] But
there is also the other model, which no longer sees
the "insignificant" detail as a trace that allows a
process to be reconstituted, but as the direct mark
of an inarticulatable truth whose imprint on the
surface of the work undoes the logic of a well-
arranged story and a rational composition of
elements. It is this second model for analyzing
details that certain art historians will later cham-
pion in opposition to the privilege that Panofsky
gave to the analysis of painting on the basis of the
story represented or the text illustrated. This
polemic, carried on in the past by Louis Marin and
today by Georges Didi-Huberman, stands under
the authority of Freud – the Freud inspired by
Morelli – as the founder of a mode of reading that
locates the truth of painting in the details of individual works: an insignificant broken column in

[17] Carlo Ginzburg, "Clues: Roots of an Evidential Paradigm," in
Clues, Myths, and the Historical Method, trans. John and Anne
Tedeschi (Baltimore: The Johns Hopkins University Press, 1989),
pp. 96–125.

Giorgione's *Tempest*, or splotches of color imitating marble on the base of Fra Angelico's *Madonna of the Shadows*.[18] Such details function as part-objects, fragments that are impossible to integrate and that undo the order of representation, legitimizing an unconscious truth not to be found in an individual history but rather in the opposition between two orders: the *figural* beneath the *figurative* or the *visual* beneath the represented *visible*. But what is today hailed as psychoanalysis's contribution to the reading of painting and its unconscious is something that Freud himself wanted nothing to do with. Nor did he have any truck with all the Medusa's heads, representatives of castration, that so many contemporary commentators have managed to discover in every head of Holofernes or John the Baptist, in some particular detail of Ginevra de' Benci's hair or an individual vortex drawn in Leonardo's notebooks.

[18] Louis Marin, *On Representation*, trans. Catherine Porter (Stanford: Stanford University Press, 2001); Georges Didi-Huberman, *Confronting Images: Questioning the Ends of a Certain History of Art*, trans. John Goodman (University Park: Pennsylvania State University Press, 2005).

It is clear that this psychoanalysis of da Vinci, as practiced notably by Louis Marin, is not the same as Freud's. It might be argued that what interests Freud in the detail privileged in this way is another truth of the painted or sculpted figure, that of the history of a singular subject, symptom, or fantasy, and that what he is looking for is the fantasy that provides the matrix of an artist's creativity, not the unconscious figural order of art. The example of *Moses*, however, runs against this simple explanation. While the statue is indeed what interests him, the principle of this interest is surprising. The long analysis of the detail of the position of the hands and the beard does not reveal any childhood secret or encrypted unconscious thought. It poses instead the most classic of questions: exactly what moment of the biblical story does Michelangelo's statue represent? Is it indeed that of Moses' fury? Is he in the act of dropping the Tablets of the Law? Here Freud is as far as possible from the analyses of Louis Marin. We could even say that in the debate between Worringer, who tried to identify different visual orders that could be correlated with dominant psychological traits, and Panofsky, who made the identification of forms secondary to that of the subjects and episodes represented, Freud de facto takes Panofsky's side. More fundamentally, his attention to detail refers to the logic of the representative order in which the plastic form was the imitation of a narrated action and the particular subject of the painting was identical with the representation of the "pregnant moment" in which the movement and meaning of the action is condensed. Freud deduces this moment from the position of the right hand and the Tablets. It is not the moment when Moses is about to strike out in indignation against the idolaters. The moment for Freud is that of anger mastered, when the hand lets go of the beard and firmly grasps the Tablets once again. This moment is not, of course, to be found in the text of the Bible. Freud adds it in the name of a rationalist interpretation in which the man who is master of himself wins out over the servant of the jealous God. The attention to detail in the end serves to identify Moses' position as

66

On Various Uses of Detail

testimony to the triumph of the will. Michelangelo's *Moses* is interpreted by Freud as something
like Winckelmann's *Laocoon*, the expression of
the victory of classical serenity over emotion. In
the case of Moses, it is specifically religious *pathos*
that is conquered by reason. Moses is the hero of
emotion conquered and brought to order. It is not
particularly important whether, as a certain tradition has it, what the Roman marble really represents for the patriarch of psychoanalysis is his
own attitude with respect to his rebellious disci-
ples. Much more than a circumstantial self-
portrait, this Moses reproduces a classical scene of
the representative age: whether it be on the tragic
stage, in *opera seria* or history painting, the
triumph of will and consciousness incarnated by a
Roman hero who reasserts his mastery of himself
and the universe: Brutus or Augustus, Scipio or
Titus. As the incarnation of victorious consciousness, Freud's Moses stands in opposition not so
much to idolaters or dissidents as to those who
have produced nothing and remained victims of
unexplicated fantasy. We are of course thinking of

67

Michelangelo's legendary *alter ego*, Leonardo da Vinci, the man of notebooks and sketches, the inventor of a thousand unrealized projects, the painter who never manages to individualize figures and always paints the same smile, in short, the man bound to his fantasy and stuck in a homosexual relation to the Father.

8 | A Conflict between Two Kinds of Medicine

There is another "figure of stone" that can be set in opposition to this classical Moses: the bas-relief of *Gradiva*. Freud judges the similarity of gait between the stone figure and the living young woman – together with the encounter of Zoe in Pompeii – to be the only "invented" and "arbitrary" element in the presentation of Norbert Hanold's case.[19] I would happily say the opposite. This young Roman virgin whose graceful gait is composed of suspended flight and firm touch on the ground, this expression of lively action and tranquil repose is anything but an arbitrary invention of Wilhelm Jensen's brain. On the contrary, we can clearly recognize a figure celebrated hundreds of times in the age of Schiller and

[19] Freud, *Jensen's "Gradiva," Standard Edition*, vol. 9, pp. 41–2.

Byron, Hölderlin and Hegel. The whole age took this image of the *kore* from Grecian urns and their memories of the *Panathenaia* frieze and built upon it their dream of a new idea of the sensible community, of a life at one with art and an art at one with life. More than an extravagant young scholar, Norbert Hanold is one of the innumerable victims, whether in a tragic or comic mode, of a certain theoretical fantasy: the quivering life of the statue, of the fold of the tunic or the free gait that incarnated the ideal world of a living community. The "fantast" Jensen finds it amusing to confront in this way the dreamed "life" of antique stone and the community-to-come with the triviality of petit-bourgeois life: neighbors, canaries in the windows, and passers-by in the street. The lover of life-incarnated-in-stone is called back to the life of prosaic and mean-spirited neighbors and the banality of petit-bourgeois honeymoons in Italy. Freud constructs his interpretation in opposition to Zoe's cure, which simply liquidates the dream in this way and leaves no place for emotional *katharsis*. He denounces the complicity between the position of the fantast and a certain prosaic end of the dream. This denunciation itself is not new. We might recall here the pages of Hegel's *Lectures on Aesthetics* where he denounces the arbitrary character of Jean-Paul or Tieck's "fancy" and its ultimate solidarity with the philistinism of bourgeois life. In both cases what is denounced is a certain use of romantic wit (*Witz*) by the "fantast." But within this proximity an essential reversal has occurred. Hegel contrasts the subjective frivolity of *Witz* with the substantial reality of mind. Freud reproaches the fantast for his failure to recognize the substantiality of the play of *Witz*. Hegel's primary concern is to set aside an empty figure of "free" subjectivity, reduced to its repetitive self-affirmation. Freud, confronted with the new developments of the aesthetic unconscious, seeks above all to put into question a certain idea of objectivity that is summarized by the idea of the "wisdom of life." In the case of the laughing Zoe Bertgang and the "fantast" Wilhelm Jensen, this wisdom looks fairly anodyne. But this is not the case in some other "cures," other ways of "ending dreams" illustrated by the literary "medicine" of the late nineteenth century. Here we might think of two exemplary fictions, one invented by a doctor's son and the other taking a doctor as its hero. The first is the conclusion of the *Sentimental Education* with its evocation of the failed visit to La Turque's bordello, which, in the collapse of both their idealistic hopes and their positive ambitions, represents the best of Frédéric's and Deslauriers's lives. Even more significant, no doubt, is the end of Zola's *Doctor Pascal*, which is also the conclusion of the whole Rougon-Macquart cycle and its moral. This moral is unique, to say the least: *Doctor Pascal* recounts the incestuous love affair between the old doctor, who is also the family historiographer, and his niece Clothilde. At the end of the book, after Pascal's death, Clothilde breastfeeds the child who is the result of this incest in the former doctor's office that has now become a nursery. The child, in his innocence of any cultural taboo, raises his little fist not to some glorious future but simply to the blind and brute force of life assuring its own perpetuity. This triumph of life, affirmed by a banal and even regenerative incest, represents the "serious" and scandalous version of Jensen's lighthearted fantasy (*fantaisie*). Zola's moral represents precisely the "bad" incest that Freud refuses: bad not because it shocks morality but because it is disconnected from any good plot based on causality – and culpability – and therefore from any logic of liberating knowledge.

I do not know whether Freud ever read *Doctor Pascal*. He certainly did read, however, and with care, the works of one of Zola's contemporaries, Ibsen, the author of exemplary histories of the soul's troubles and of childhood secrets, cures, confessions, and healings. Freud gives an analysis of his play *Rosmersholm* in the essay "Some Character-Types Met with in Psycho-analytic Work." This text studies a paradoxical group of patients who are opposed to the rationality of the psycho-analytic cure: some because they refuse to renounce a satisfaction and to submit the pleasure principle to the reality principle; others, to the contrary, because they flee from their own success and refuse a satisfaction at the very moment they can obtain it, when it is no longer marked by the seal of impossibility or transgression. Such are the young lady who has long schemed her marriage and the professor who is about to obtain the chair for which he has long intrigued, and who flee from the success of their enterprise. Freud's interpretation is that the possibility of success provokes the invasion of an uncontrollable feeling of culpability. At this point he brings in examples drawn from two exemplary plays: *Macbeth*, of course, but also *Rosmersholm*. Since Ibsen's play is less well known than Shakespeare's, it is worthwhile to summarize the plot. The setting is an old manor house located on the outskirts of a small town in Norway, huddled at the end of a fjord. In this manor, connected to the world by a footbridge crossing a turbulent mill-race, lives the former pastor Rosmer, the heir to a long family of local notables. A year before the action of the play, his wife, suffering from mental illness, threw herself into the water. In the same house lives the governess Rebecca, who came there after the death of her stepfather, Dr West. This free-thinker had educated Rebecca after her mother's death and converted her to his liberal ideas. Rosmer's cohabitation with the young woman has two consequences. First, the former pastor is converted to liberal ideas, which he publicly endorses, to the great scandal of his brother-in-law, headmaster Kroll, the leader of the local party of order. Secondly, his intellectual community with Rebecca is transformed into feelings of love, and he proposes marriage to her. But Rebecca, after a momentary reaction of joy, declares marriage impossible. Whereupon headmaster Kroll arrives to reveal to his brother-in-law that his wife was driven to suicide and to Rebecca that her birth was illegitimate: she is in fact the natural child of her "stepfather." Rebecca energetically refuses to believe this. She admits, however, that she was the one who had insinuated into the dead woman's mind the ideas that drove her to suicide. She then prepares to leave the manor, at which point Rosmer again asks her to become his wife. She refuses once again, saying she is no longer the ambitious young woman who had moved into the house and quietly gotten rid of the wife who stood in her way. If knowing her has converted Rosmer to free thought, she on the contrary has been ennobled by contact with him. She can no longer enjoy the success she has won.

It is here that Freud intervenes, once again with the goal of correcting the explanations given by the author and reestablishing the true etiology of the case. According to Freud, the moral reason invoked by Rebecca is merely a screen. The young woman herself indicates a more solid reason: she has "a past." And it is easy to understand what this past is by analyzing her reaction to the revelation about her birth. If she refuses so energetically to admit that she is West's daughter, and if the consequence of this revelation is to make her confess her criminal maneuvers, it is because she was this so-called stepfather's lover. The recognition of incest is what sets off the feeling of guilt; it, and not her moral conversion, stands in the way of Rebecca's success. In order to understand her behavior we must reestablish the truth that the play does not tell and could not tell other than by vague allusions.[20]

But when he opposes this "true" hidden reason to the "moralizing" one declared by the heroine, Freud forgets what gives Rebecca's behavior its final meaning in Ibsen's eyes. He forgets the end of the play, where neither moralizing conversion nor the crushing weight of guilt is operative. Rebecca's transformation is located beyond good and evil and is manifested not by a conversion to morality but by the impossibility of acting, the impossibility of willing even. For Rebecca who no longer wants to act and Rosmer who no longer wants to know, the story ends in a particular kind of mystical union. They unite and march joyously toward the footbridge where they drown together in the coursing water. This ultimate union of knowledge and non-knowledge, of activity and passivity, fully expresses the logic of the aesthetic unconscious. The true cure, the true healing, is Schopenhauerian renunciation of the will to live,

[20] Freud, "Some Character-Types Met with in Psycho-analytic Work," *Standard Edition*, vol. 14, p. 329.

self-abandon to the original sea of non-willing, the "supreme bliss" into which Wagner's Isolde descended and that the young Nietzsche assimilated to the triumph of a new Dionysos.

Such bliss is what Freud refuses. Against it he puts forward the good causal plot, the rationality of the feeling of guilt liberated by headmaster Kroll's cure. It is not the moralizing explanation but the "innocence" of plunging into the primordial sea that he opposes. Here again the ambiguity of Freud's relation to the aesthetic unconscious appears in stark relief: faced with this nihilism, this radical identity of *pathos* and *logos* that, in the age of Ibsen, Strindberg, and Wagnerism, became the ultimate truth and the "moral" of the aesthetic unconscious, Freud retreats to what is in the end the position adopted by Corneille and Voltaire when confronted with Oedipus's fury. He seeks to reestablish, against this *pathos*, a good causal concatenation and a positive virtue that would be the effect of knowledge. The force of what is at stake here for Freud can be felt in a brief reference to another of Ibsen's "psychoanalytic" dramas, *The Lady from the Sea*, in which Dr Wangel's wife is haunted by the irresistible call of the sea. When her husband leaves her free to follow the passing sailor in whom she recognizes the incarnation of this call, Ellida renounces her desire. Just as Rebecca claimed that contact with Rosmer has transformed her, Ellida claims to have been set free by the choice her husband gave her. Since she can choose, she will stay with him. This time, however, the relation between the author's reasons and the interpreter's appear in an inverse relation. Freud confirms the character's interpretation and sees it as a successful "cure" carried out by Dr Wangel. Ibsen's preparatory notes, however, reduce this freedom to an illusory status; the plot summary he gives is resolutely Schopenhauerian:

> Life is apparently a happy, easy, and lively
> thing up there in the shadow of the mountains
> and in the monotony of this seclusion. Then
> the suggestion is thrown up that this kind of
> life is a life of shadows. No initiative; no fight

for liberty. Only longings and desires. This is how life is lived in the brief light summer. And afterwards – into the darkness. Then longings are roused for the life of the great world outside. But what would be gained from that? With changed surroundings and with one's mind developed, there is an increase in one's cravings and longings and desires. [. . .] Everywhere limitation. From this comes melancholy like a subdued song of mourning over the whole of human existence and all the activities of men. One bright summer day with a great darkness thereafter – that is all. [. . .] The sea's power of attraction. The longing for the sea. People akin to the sea. Bound by the sea. Dependent on the sea. Must return to it. [. . .] The great secret is the dependence of the human will upon "the will-less."[21]

Thus the cycle of seasons in the north is identified with the vanishing of the illusions of representation

[21] Henrik Ibsen, Draft for *The Lady from the Sea*, in *The Oxford Ibsen*, ed. James Walter McFarlane (London: Oxford University Press, 1966), vol. 7, pp. 449–50.

into the nothingness of the will that wills nothing. In this case Freud adopts Dr Wangel's and the Lady from the Sea's moral in opposition to the one proposed by the author.

We might consider this to be a "historical" issue, but this does not mean that there is anything circumstantial about it. Freud was not simply fighting against an ideology present in the spirit of the age – an age, moreover, that was already receding into the past when he wrote these texts. The battle is between two versions of the unconscious, two ideas of what lies beneath the polite, polished surface of societies, two ideas of civilization's ills and the way to heal them. Since we are speaking of periods, let us note precisely when this one is located. *The Moses of Michelangelo* was written in 1914; both *The Uncanny* and the short text on Ibsen in 1915. We are not far from the turning point in Freud's work constituted by the introduction of the death drive in *Beyond the Pleasure Principle*. Freud himself explained this turn in his work in terms of the deduction of the death drive from the study of the problematic "traumatic neurosis." But its recognition is also bound to the blow that the war of 1914 delivered to the optimistic vision that had guided the first era of psychoanalysis and the simple opposition between pleasure principle and reality principle. There are, however, reasons to suspect that this explanation does not exhaust the significance of this moment. The discovery of the death drive is also an episode in Freud's long and often disguised confrontation with the great obsessive theme of the epoch in which psychoanalysis was formed: the unconscious of the Schopenhauerian thing-in-itself and the great literary fictions of return to this unconscious. The ultimate secret of the whole tradition of the novel of the illusions of the will, summarizing the literature of a century, the literature of the aesthetic age, is that what life-preserving instincts ultimately preserve for life is its movement toward "its" death and that the "guardians of life" are in fact "myrmidons of death." Freud never stopped fighting with this secret. Indeed, the interpretation of the "reality principle" lies at the heart of the corrections Freud makes to Jensen's, Hoffmann's, or Ibsen's plots. This confrontation with the logic of the aesthetic unconscious is what compels him to reestablish the correct etiology of Hanold or Nathaniel's case and the proper ending to *Rosmersholm*, but also the correct attitude of Moses, that of the calm victory of reason over sacred passion. Everything occurs as if these analyses were so many ways of resisting the nihilist entropy that Freud detects and rejects in the works of the aesthetic regime of art, but that he will also legitimize in his theorization of the death drive.

We are now in a position to understand the paradoxical relation between Freud's aesthetic analyses and those that will later claim his patronage. The intention of the latter is to refute Freud's biographism and his indifference to artistic "form." They look for the effect of the unconscious in the particularities of pictorial touch that silently belie the figurative anecdote or in the "stammerings" of the literary text that mark the action of "another language" within language. Understood in this way as the stamp of an unnamable truth or the shock produced by the force of the Other, the unconscious exceeds in principle any adequate sensible presentation. At the beginning of *The Moses*, Freud evokes the shock provoked by great works and the disarray that can seize hold of thought confronted with the enigma of this shock. "Possibly, indeed, some writer on aesthetics has discovered that this state of intellectual bewilderment is a necessary condition when a great work of art is to achieve its greatest effects. It would only be with the greatest reluctance that I could bring myself to believe in any such necessity."[22] The mainspring of Freud's analyses, the reason for the privilege he gives to the biographical plot, whether it be the biography of the fictional character or of the artist, can be found in the fact that he refuses to ascribe the power of painting, sculpture, or literature to this bewilderment. In order to refute the thesis of this hypothetical aesthetician, Freud is ready to revise any story and if necessary even rewrite the sacred text. But the aesthetician who

[22] Freud, *The Moses of Michelangelo, Standard Edition*, vol. 13, pp. 211–12.

was a hypothesis for Freud is today an actual figure in the field of aesthetic thought. As a general rule he relies precisely on Freud to provide the grounding for the thesis that his patron wanted to refute, the thesis that links the work's power to its bewildering effect. I have in mind here most particularly the analyses in which Jean-François Lyotard, toward the end of his life, elaborated an aesthetics of the sublime whose three pillars are Burke, Kant, and Freud.[23] Lyotard contrasts the weak-mindedness of aesthetics with the power of the pictorial touch conceived as a power of divestiture. The subject, disarmed by the stamp of the *aistheton*, the sensible that affects the naked soul, is confronted with a power of the Other, which in the final instance is the face of God that no one can look upon, putting the spectator in the position of Moses before the burning bush. Against Freudian sublimation Lyotard poses this stamp of

[23] See Jean-François Lyotard, *The Inhuman: Reflections on Time*, trans. Geoffrey Bennington and Rachel Bowlby (Stanford: Stanford University Press, 1992), and *Postmodern Fables*, trans. Georges Van Den Abbeele (Minneapolis: University of Minnesota Press, 1997).

the sublime, producing the triumph of a *pathos* irreducible to any *logos*, a *pathos* that in the final analysis is identified with the power of God himself calling Moses.

The relation between the two versions of the unconscious then takes the shape of a singular crisscross. Freudian psychoanalysis presupposes the aesthetic revolution that rescinds the causal order of classical representation and identifies the power of art with the immediate identity of contraries, of *logos* and *pathos*. It presupposes a literature based on the twofold power of mute speech. But Freud makes a choice within this duality. Against the nihilist entropy inherent in the power of voiceless speech, Freud chooses the other form of mute speech, the hieroglyph offered to the labor of interpretation and the hope of healing. Following this logic, he tends to assimilate the work of "fantasy" and the labor of its deciphering with the classical plot of recognition that the aesthetic revolution had rejected. He thus brings back within the frame of the representative regime of art the figures and plot structures that this old regime had rejected and that it took the aesthetic revolution to put at his disposal. Today, a different Freudianism argues against this return. It puts into question Freudian biographism and claims to be more respectful of the specificity of art. It presents itself as a more radical Freudianism in that it has been freed from the sequels of the representative tradition and harmonized with the new regime of art that made Oedipus available, the new regime that equates activity and passivity by affirming both the anti-representative auton-omy of art *and* its forcibly heteronomic nature, its value as testimony to the action of forces that go beyond the subject and tear it away from itself. In order to do this, of course, it relies above all on *Beyond the Pleasure Principle* and other texts of the 1920s and 1930s that mark the distance Freud has taken from the corrector of Jensen, Ibsen, and Hoffmann, from the Freud who admired Moses for having freed himself from sacred fury. This project requires a decision within the contradic-tory logic of the aesthetic unconscious, within the polarity of mute speech, opposite to the one made by Freud. The voiceless power of the Other's speech must be valorized as something irreducible to any hermeneutics. This requires in turn an assumption of the whole nihilist entropy, even at the cost of transforming the bliss of returning to the original abyss into a sacred relation to the Other and the Law. This Freudianism then executes a turning movement around Freud's theory, bringing back in Freud's name and against him the nihilism that his aesthetic analyses never stopped fighting against. This turning movement affirms itself as a rejection of the aesthetic tradition.[24] But it might in fact be the final trick that the aesthetic unconscious plays on the Freudian unconscious.

[24] See Lyotard, "Anima Minima," in *Postmodern Fables*, pp. 235–49.

Index

Index

Index

Index